From **Bean** to **Brew**

A History of Coffee and Coffeehouses

Gary Michael Smith

From Bean To Brew

Other Titles From Chatgris Press

The Peer-Reviewed Journal: A Comprehensive Guide through the Editorial Process

Publishing for Small Press Runs. How to Print and Market from 20 to 200 Copies of Your Book

Guided Meditation. Creative Visualization for Generating Energy and Managing Stress

The Complete Guide to Driving Etiquette. Taking the Rules of the Road a Step Further

Angelina's Favorite Recipes. A Personal Collection of Sicilian Style Italian Recipes

The Veranda. The Stage for the Storyteller

All books are available from online booksellers such as amazon.com, barnesandnoble.com, and borders.com. Books also are available from the publisher at Chatgris Press, P.O. Box 15092, New Orleans, LA 70175-5092. An order form appears in the back of this book.

From Bean to Brew

A History of Coffee and Coffeehouses

Second Edition

Gary Michael Smith

Chatgris Press
New Orleans

From Bean to Brew

Chatgris Press
P.O. Box 15092
New Orleans, LA 70175-5092
504-895-5219
504-895-2352 fax
gsmith@comm.net
www.ChatgrisPress.com

Printed in the United States of America

Second Edition

10 9 8 7 6 5 4 3 2

ISBN 0-9658380-9-9

Front cover images complements of Dr. Robert A. Rice of the Smithsonian Migratory Bird Center at the National Zoological Park in Washington, DC.

Back cover photograph complements of Brenda Joy Floyd.

This book was developed using Microsoft Word 2000 on Windows 98. Text reproduction was provided by *Print*TECH of Metairie, LA (www.printtechonline.com), the cover was designed by Gary Michael Smith, and the digital offset printing for the cover was provided by Garrison Digital Color, Inc. of New Orleans, LA (www.gdci.com).

Contents

Tables

To Boris, Beet, Sylvester, and Chatgris who, although they don't drink coffee, are loved nonetheless.

Acknowledgments

I am eternally grateful to everyone who participated in my persistent interviews, discussions, and nonstop queries about coffeehouses and the coffee industry. I toast them with a double grande latte.

Special thanks go to Dr. Robert A. Rice, Policy Research Scientist at the Smithsonian Migratory Bird Center at the National Zoo in Washington, DC, for permitting the use of his slides 13 (coffee flowers) and 14 (coffee cherries) for the cover design. See www.si.edu/smbc/coffee.htm for the complete slide presentation.

Much thanks also go to Julia Cates for her never-ending artistic and creative insight, and to Dean M. Shapiro who used his expertise in grammar and history to skillfully edit this text.

From the Author

This book represents a collection of facts (and some legend) on the history and popularity of coffee and coffeehouses. This research by no means represents a complete description of coffees, equipment, or coffeehouses; the reader is referred to the References and Contacts sections for more detailed information.

When I began research on this project, only a handful gourmet coffeehouses existed in New Orleans. Consequently, the focus of my early research depended largely on personal experiences and explorations while traveling throughout Europe, Mexico, and six provinces of Canada. And it was the U.S. Pacific Northwest that offered a plethora of resources since this area is considered by some to be the "founder of the gourmet coffeehouse" industry.

Throughout the 1990s, New Orleanians' love of coffee helped coffeehouses in The Big Easy grow at a phenomenal rate. (The prominence of being the home of the world's largest bulk handling plant didn't hurt either.) Independent houses opened across the city, and chains were formed and sold an abundance of successful franchises. Outside chains also took advantage of the growing market for coffeehouses in the Crescent City.

I hope you find the historic and contemporary information in *From Bean to Brew* interesting and thought provoking.

From Bean to Brew

Part One

A History
Lesson

From Bean to Brew

Threw role of coffeehouses in modern America has been one of artistic as well as commercial cooperation between patrons and entrepreneurs alike. One function that many coffeehouses provide today is that of offering a nonalcoholic alternative form of socializing in a time of widespread promotion of alcohol consumption.

Another function is to offer artistic expression, in front of an audience, in the form of literary readings, art exhibits, theatrical performances, video and film screenings, fashion shows, and musical performances covering the spectrum of jazz, gospel, bluegrass, old-time country, pop, rock, and blues.

Coffeehouses in Europe have been a mainstay in these relaxed cultures for centuries. And barring the beatniks and hippies of the 1950s and 1960s in San Francisco and Greenwich Village, it has only been since the 1980s that socializing in this venue has once again seen such a phenomenal resurgence throughout contemporary America. In fact, popularity is so widespread that today coffee is second only to oil as the largest traded commodity in the world.

The History of Coffee

The names for coffee in almost every country are descended from the Arabian word *qahwa*, meaning "that gives strength," and its Turkish derivative, *kahveh*. The French and Spanish *café*, Italian *caffè*, German *kaffee*, Finnish *kahvi*, Dutch *koffie*, Greek *kafes*, and others are all phonetic approximations of the original Arabic or Turkish words. By 1650, the words *coffey* and *coffee* developed from these names, and by 1700 the single word "coffee" had become the standard term.

The story of coffee is claimed by legend to begin

around 800 A.D. with Kaldi, a young goat- or sheepherder in the hills of Yemen on the Arabian Peninsula across from Ethiopia. Kaldi was puzzled by the curious behavior of his animals; every morning they would flock to the many evergreen shrubs scattered throughout the pasture. And these particular bushes were laden with clumps of red berries. After a brief time, the animals would begin to frolic—uncontrollably. Overtaken with curiosity, Kaldi tried the berries himself and soon was dancing as well.

Meanwhile, the monks living in the hills observed this morning ritual, and deduced that there must be something in those little red berries. They experimented, and soon discovered that if they soaked the beans in water and drank the broth, it kept them awake for hours during nightly prayers.

This goat story may or may not be true, but according to history, coffee was being cultivated in Yemen as long ago as the 6th century. And by the 9th century the Arabs were using coffee beans for nutritional and medicinal purposes.

After coffee's emergence in Arabia, its production was kept under watchful eyes; although Arabia willingly exported large quantities, they nonetheless guarded its cultivation. At 1 to 2 pounds of ground coffee per tree, coffee was extremely valuable. And even though a coffee tree can produce for 40 to 50 years, the greatest produce is yielded between the age of 5 to 13 years.

The Arabs' cautiousness, however, was a losing struggle with European botanists who spied on these Arabian plantation activities. By 1690, the Dutch succeeded in transporting plants out of Arabia and into botanical gardens in Holland. They also began cultivation on the Indonesian island of Java, and in 1706 Javanese coffee arrived in Amsterdam. Thereafter, the Dutch sent coffee plants to botanical gardens throughout Europe.

A History Lesson

In 17th century Paris, King Louis XIV tried some of the brew during one of his trading trips to Yemen and immediately fell in love with it. The Dutch, wanting to please the coffee-loving king, presented him with a single coffee tree. By the 18th century, Dutch coffee was a bartered luxury in homes in the remote Highland sea lochs of Scotland.

Back in Paris, a government botanist constructed a hot house where the heat and humidity replicated the Yemen climate. To begin the cultivation, a seedling coffee tree was shipped in the early 1720s to the French island colony of Martinique (today, the honorary sister city of New Orleans) in the Caribbean where the French had land and trade interests. But turbulent storms almost destroyed the ship, and most of the cargo was lost. Captain Gabriel Mathieu de Clieu, however, knew the importance of the small freight, and protected the seedling until they reached the island. This seedling, and its progeny, eventually became the rootstock for all South American coffees.

While these French/South American plants were still in the early growing phases, the Dutch already had been quite successful in growing coffee on Java. The French, having a trade route that stopped on the island, then began shipping from Java. With this new source of coffee at a cheaper price than in Yemen—and with the developing coffee plantations on Bourbon—France's love for coffee grew wildly.

When the emissaries of King Louis the XIV arrived on the lower Mississippi River in North America, they founded an intense shipping port they called New Orleans. One of the first ships to be unloaded, directly across the street from what was in contemporary New Orleans Kaldi's Coffeehouse and Coffeemuseum, carried bags of coffee from two ports: the Yemen port of Mocha and the Indonesian island of Java. In New Orleans, these two

5

coffees were blended together, and the resulting Mocha Java became an instant hit.

The History of Coffeehouses

When and where the first coffeehouse was opened is widely disputed. One theory is that during the 1683 siege of Vienna, Austria, the Viennese burned what they thought was camel fodder left behind by the retreating Turks. A well-trained interpreter/courier/spy and officer with the liberating Polish army realized from the aroma that what they were burning were sacks of green coffee beans.

Franciszek Jerzy Kulczycki (alternate spelling Franz Georg Kolschitzky) claimed the sacks of coffee from the city council as his reward for leading the Polish Army to the rescue of the city. Kulczycki eventually founded what is believed to be central Europe's first *kaffeehaus* in Vienna called The Blue Bottle. He also is credited with refining the brewing method by filtering out the grounds, and sweetening and adding milk—giving birth to Viennese coffee.

Another theory regarding the first Viennese coffee house purports that, although Venice received its first shipment of green coffee beans in 1615, the first establishment that served its brew, Caffè Florian, did not open until 68 years later in 1683.

Today, there are more than 800 coffeehouses in the city. And even though the name of an establishment often is written as two words, "coffeehouse" is the first (preferred) listing in Webster's II New Riverside University Dictionary, indicating that, perhaps, the one-word term has worked its way into our lexicon.

Another theory regarding the first coffeehouse is based on records in Edinburgh, Scotland. These archives chronicle that John's Coffee House, popularly known as

"Peaches," opened in the Piazza at the northeast of Parliament Close in 1688.

In Paris, Francesco Procopio de Coltelli of Sicily opened Le Procope in 1686. Considered to be one of the first cafés, it is reported still in business today. Such cafés are credited with fostering the intellectual ferment that led to the French Revolution; in 1843 there were more than 3,000 cafés in Paris alone. These first coffeehouses tended to attract people of high social standing, such as poets, painters, sculptors, and politicians. It also is reported that one café in Paris premiered the world's first motion picture.

The popularity of coffeehouses spread to London, with the number of coffeehouses multiplying enormously during the Restoration. By 1700, there were nearly 2,000 coffeehouses in London, or one for every 300 to 400 Londoners. It also is suggested that within the coffeehouses in England, the practice of tipping wait staff began. Patrons wanting better service and seating put money into a tin can labeled "To Insure Prompt Service."

Individual coffeehouses became known for the type of business that was conducted under their roofs. Lloyd's of London originated with Edward Lloyd's Coffee House in Change Alley near the Thames on Tower Street in 1687, and it became so popular that it had to be moved to larger quarters on Lombard Street. Also, Jonathan's Coffee House was the motivator behind the London Stock Exchange. In 1760, a group of 150 brokers formed a club at Jonathan's Coffee House to meet, and to buy and sell shares. In 1773, the members of this club voted to change the name of Jonathan's to the Stock Exchange.

The first record of someone imbibing in coffee in England is said to have happened in 1637 when a Cretan scholar named Canopius brewed a cup in his chambers at Balliol College. The first coffeehouse in England is said to have opened in Oxford in 1650 by a Turkish Jew named Jacob.

Coffeehouses in England became an integral part of intellectual, social, and commercial life, attracting an eclectic group who enjoyed intellectualizing on numerous topics regarding literary, political, and mercantile affairs. Also, the rise in coffeehouses corresponded with the rise of the London press, and people could read newspapers at the houses.

King Charles II even noticed, to his disapproval, that both upper and lower classes were intermingling. Consequently, he referred to these places as "penny universities" because not only were patrons getting more (and more accurate) news here from local papers, notices, bulletins, and gossip, a penny was the price of a cup of coffee.

Coffeehouses also were convenient centers for sending and receiving mail in days when government efforts to develop a postal system were futile because of the absence of street numbers. It is from these fragments of history that the Penny Post Coffeehouse (now called the Neutral Ground Coffee House) in New Orleans most likely acquired its name.

Although we associate the contemporary coffeehouse with relaxation, this image is not universal. For instance, in some establishments in Italy, patrons often opt to stand at a counter, balancing a demitasse cup and baked pastries, instead of paying double for the privilege of sitting at a table. Luckily, coffeehouses in the United States usually do not operate on such a two-tier system. Here, patrons can expect to sit, relax, and enjoy a peaceful cup of java.

Even though traditional coffeehouses today are specialty shops serving gourmet coffees and teas, in colonial America the coffeehouse was actually a combination tavern/inn/coffeehouse where coffee, tea, ale, and rum were consumed. Coffeehouses in modern America, though, also can include sleek, high-profile spaces. These nouveau coffeehouses offer specialty coffee mainly as a tantalizing draw for business, but actually prefer to sell to a crowd interested in a more substantial variety of cuisine and, in some establishments, alcohol.

Early Opposition

Historically, acceptance of this new stimulating beverage was not worldwide. From the 13th to 15th centuries, coffeehouses in some areas were labeled as dens of immorality and vice. One punishment mandated by the Grand Vizier Kuprili of the Turkish Ottoman Empire for those who violated his restriction on coffeehouses was severe beatings for the first offense; the second offense entailed being sewn into a leather bag and thrown into a river. Harsher treatments also were administered. In the 16th and 17th centuries, anyone caught drinking coffee in Turkey was put to death.

In 1600, priests in Italy asked Pope Clement VIII to forbid coffee. After trying the drink, however, he baptized it instead, declaring it a Christian beverage. After such a prominent endorsement, coffee experienced widespread growth, and become known in 15th century Mecca as the "drink of Islam."

In 1674 London, women complained that their husbands were never home because they were always in coffeehouses. Consequently, they circulated The Women's Petition Against Coffee, which protested "the grand inconveniences accruing to their sex from the excessive use of the drying and enfeebling liquor." In response, King Charles II attempted to place a ban on coffeehouses, but was forced to reverse his decision only 16 days later because of public outcry against the ban.

Frederick The Great of Prussia also attempted to condemn the consumption of coffee by blocking imports in 1775. He even dispatched coffee smellers to sniff the streets in search of outlawed home roasting. Again, public dissention prevailed.

Early Coffee Making

Street vending has its beginnings in 17th century Europe when coffee merchants, called "aquacedratjos," actually wore on their clothing all the paraphernalia needed to prepare and serve a fresh cup of coffee. The aquacedratjos peddled their brew from house to house, giving their patrons the choice of using their own cups or those of the vendor.

By the mid-1800s coffee had become so popular that cafés could not keep up with the demand. To help meet the public's mania, the first espresso machines—which forced hot water through the grounds using steam instead of letting it drip through—were invented by either Louis Bernard Rabaut or Michel Varnier sometime around 1822 in France. And at the Paris Exposition of 1855, Edward Loysel de Santais unveiled his coffee machine astounding the crowds by producing 2,000 cups of bad coffee in 1 hour.

By 1903, a gentleman in Milan by the name of Bezzara introduced the first commercially manufactured machine that could make espresso, although it was not until 1946 that Achille Gaggia designed the prototype for today's machines. As with the 1822 machine, the Gaggia machine also used hot water under pressure rather than steam, producing a smooth, rich cup of espresso.

Early Coffeehouses of New Orleans

Perhaps the reason New Orleans got its reputation as a coffee-consuming capital is because coffee is not a new beverage to this area. Early records show that in 1802 New Orleans, 1,438 bags of coffee were imported from Latin America. And this number grew to 530,000 bags by 1857. Moreover, the 1858 city directory listed more than 500 coffeehouses in New Orleans. Consequently, it is no wonder that in the 1840s, New Orleans was the second largest port in the country—with New York being first— and the fourth largest in the world.

New Orleanians took full advantage of this standing. A coffee break was scheduled daily from 1800 to 1860 where Creole bankers, brokers, importers, and exporters conducted business on Exchange Alley in the French Quarter in "exchanges," as coffeehouses were called.

It was in this area—from Canal Street to the Place d' Armes (today's Jackson Square)—that in 1859 the Sazerac Coffee House was opened by importer John B. Schiller. The coffeehouse was located at 13 Exchange Alley and was named after Schiller's favorite brand of cognac.

Another of the original coffeehouses in this city, Café du Monde, has occupied the same location on Decatur Street since 1862. And near there was one of the first coffee warehouses, where Kaldi's Coffeehouse and Coffeemuseum recently was located.

Also historic, Morning Call was established in 1870 by a Yugoslavian immigrant, Joseph Jurasich, at St. Phillip and Decatur streets. The menus of both places have remained unchanged, and although Morning Call moved to the suburb of Metairie in 1974, it still is operated by the original family—the grandson of the founder.

Even with the intense competition among the city's

brokers, importers, wholesalers, and roasters, the New Orleans Men's Association—later called the Green Coffee Association—was formed and held its first meeting at Galatoire's restaurant on December 20, 1915.

Thus, the coffee industry was well established in the city by the turn of the century. And by 1942, records showed that commerce was thriving in this area with 40 importers, two wholesalers, two storage companies, and eight roasters.

Part Two

Roasting, Grinding, Brewing, and Storing

From Bean to Brew

Roasting for Freshness

Today's coffee drinkers have developed a sophistication in their taste for coffee, and with competition among coffeehouses—many of which actually roast as well as grind and brew their drinks—so great, proprietors demand a high level of freshness. Many coffeehouse owners today require their suppliers to vacuum pack their beans within 30 minutes of roasting, and this coffee must be sold within 7 days or it will be thrown away. Some proprietors will even hire a personal roastmaster who is familiar with the roasting properties of the certain coffee beans offered at the owner's coffeehouse.

Coffee roasting equipment, some believe, is an essential part of the coffee business. One coffeehouse in New Orleans uses a 1928 Gothot roaster—one of about 20 in existence today—which takes between 15 and 30 minutes to roast 17 pounds of coffee. And proprietors feel that roasting such a small amount at a time, as opposed to commercial coffee roasting factories that roast many pounds at a time and use water to cool hot beans, enables roasters to more closely monitor all processes involved from roasting to air cooling.

The act of roasting is what gives the coffee its essence by transforming sugars, starches, and fats into coffee oil, which really is not an oil but some of the more than 600 compounds that have been drawn to the surface of the bean. The longer the roasting time, the greater the amount of oil brought to the surface, making the ground and brewed coffee smoother than lighter roasts, for which much of the acid is still within the bean. This is why a cup of light roast used to make espresso will be bitter.

Also, dark roast coffees—beans that have been roasted for a longer period of time—have less caffeine and acidity.

From Bean to Brew

When used to make espresso, these beans have even less than regularly brewed coffee because the process of making espresso results in leaving more caffeine in the grounds. Moreover, arabicas, which are used for espresso, contain only half the caffeine of robustas.

Home roasting, although still perhaps on the same level as home beer brewing or wine making, nonetheless is growing in popularity. Some feel there is nothing like taking green beans and personally roasting them to their own taste.

Grinding and Brewing

Grinding is an important aspect in the preparation of well-brewed coffee. The coffee for espresso is ground finer than filtered coffee, but not too finely nor too coarsely. If the coffee is ground too finely, the water will take too long to drain, making the coffee bitter; if ground too coarsely, the water will pass over the coffee too quickly, not allowing the oils to be extracted and making the coffee weak.

Moreover, the finer the grind, the greater the chance of damaging the flavor oils of the bean. In general, the grounds should be fine and gritty, but not powdery; the appropriate size could be compared with sugar or salt crystals.

Although one could use a mortar and pestle to grind beans, the preferred way today is to use a good burr grinder with a powerful, slow-speed motor that generates little heat; heat generated by grinding is an easy way to destroy the flavor of coffee. And be advised that most grocery store grinders do not grind finely enough for good espresso, even if the finest setting is selected.

Today's espresso is different from filtered coffee in several ways. Filtered coffee is a clear liquid that contains

16

only a small amount of solid material. Espresso, on the other hand, contains solids suspended in liquid, dissolved solids, and oils broken down by heat.

Many people believe that espresso is loaded with caffeine, but in reality, full caffeine extraction is impossible because of the extremely fast brewing period. The sensation of stronger coffee is a result of the reaction of the taste buds, which open much wider and faster because of the increased temperature of the liquid.

This physiological reaction enables the caffeine to enter the body quicker without the acidity (and nervousness) associated with regular coffee. Espresso—although possessing half the caffeine as regular brewed coffee— tastes stronger because it packs the same amount of coffee and suspended solids into 1 to 2 ounces of water instead of the typical 6 to 10 ounces.

Moreover, by comparison, a cup of regular robusta (supermarket) coffee contains as much as 150mg of caffeine, whereas a cup of espresso made from arabica beans has only about 60 to 90mg. And dark roast contains even less caffeine as described earlier.

Regarding temperature, an espresso machine creates a pressure of 9x gravity, and the water should be 184 to 189 degrees Fahrenheit as it leaves the spout. The water temperature in the tank meanwhile is around 230 degrees. Consequently, few home machines can perform up to the standards of commercial equipment; it would cost a consumer about $400 for an authentic home espresso outfit, unless of course you wanted to pay up to $17,000 for a hammered copper and brass Faema or a LaCimbali machine from Italy.

But even a good countertop machine can produce quality espresso and cappuccino, if operated correctly. Without going into too much detail on frothing (other texts give more, in-depth information), basic rules to follow include those listed below.

- Use only cold milk. It froths easier than warm or even room temperature milk.

- Use nonfat or fat-free milk for a stiff, dry foam, or 2 percent or whole milk for a smoother, creamier, longer-lasting head.

- Use a stainless steel pitcher, not ceramic or glass. There's something about the steel vibrating while froth-ing that makes the task easier.

With regard to brewing regular coffee, remember that coffee loses its flavor quickly, so reheating on a stove or in a microwave is never recommended, unless you have a taste for stale coffee. Also, the brew basket should be removed immediately after brewing because the residual dripping coffee is bitter. Finally, impatient office workers should be discouraged from replacing the pot with their cup during the brew cycle; this disturbs the balance of the whole pot of coffee.

Storing

Storage of ground coffee or whole beans also is important to maintain the quality of the flavor. Although only whole beans should be stored, there is controversy over whether or not to freeze. Experts say that since coffee oil is water soluble, it will freeze—especially since, from the extended roasting time, much of it is on the surface of the bean. And some feel that once the oils and aromatics are congealed by being frozen, they are never the same. Some good rules of thumb for storing coffee are listed below.

- Store only the amount of beans that can be used within a week to 10 days.

- Freeze only if you plan on keeping it longer than 2 weeks.

- Do not even bother storing grounds since they begin to stale immediately after grinding and will absorb odors from the refrigerator.

To prevent freezer burn of beans, stored only in an airtight glass container; this will minimize air contamination. For the best results, though, coffee should be stored in a cool, dark, and dry place, and used within a few days.

From Bean to Brew

Part Three

Drinking
and
Enjoying

From Bean to Brew

Categories and Flavors

The two major commercial categories of coffee sold in this country are Coffea arabica and Coffea canephora (robusta), and each has its own characteristics and place of origin. Arabica beans are harder and more flavorful than robusta beans, are grown at higher altitudes, and used to make the gourmet coffees. The robusta bean is less fragile, hardier, less expensive, and as mentioned earlier contains twice the caffeine as arabicas. This is the coffee that is sold in grocery stores.

"Grading" involves such criteria as size, color, species, cup quality, the altitude at which the bean is grown, and the process used for gathering and for preparation. Some examples are displayed in tables 1 and 2 below.

Gourmet beans may differ from one another in that many are flavored. Unfortunately, these flavors do not come naturally but are given to the bean by way of a liquid flavor essence bath after roasting, whereby the bean absorbs the flavors until saturated. Moreover, some individuals cannot drink flavored coffees because of allergies to the liquid essence, which can give them headaches.

Some of the most popular flavors for coffee include French Vanilla, Amaretto, Brazilian Oro, Viennese, Toasted Almond, Irish Cream, Hazelnut Cream, Mocha Java, Southern Pecan, French Praline, and Bananas Foster. Flavored syrups also are popular in flavoring both lattes and even just steamed milk with no espresso.

But even if you cannot find your preferred flavor of bean at your favorite coffeehouse, you can buy a wide variety of whole beans at specialty coffee stores, one of which in New Orleans is the Orleans Coffee Exchange. See their site at www.OrleansCoffee.com.

ARABICA (GOURMET COFFEE)	
Location	**Coffee**
Kenya	AA
Tanzania	Kilimanjaro
Celebes (Holland)	Sulawesi
Costa Rica	Tarrazu
Guatemala	Antigua
Brazil	Bourbon Santos
Venezuela	Maracaibo, Tachira
Peru	Chanchamayo
Jamaica	Blue Mountain
Yemen	Mocha, Sanani
Hawaii	Kona
India	Mysore
El Salvador	Euro Prep
Mexico	Coatepec, High Grown Daxaca Pluma
Ethiopia	Harrar, Yergacheffe
New Guinea	"Y" Grade
Colombia	Supremo

Table 1. Arabica Coffee

ROBUSTA ("SUPERMARKET" COFFEE)	
Location	**Coffee**
Indonesia	Java
India, Uganda	Drugar, Wugar
The Ivory Coast	Grade 1

Table 2. Robusta Coffee

Orleans Coffee Exchange, located in the French Quarter beneath an apartment once occupied by playwright Tennessee Williams, offers more than 100 different flavors of coffee from 22 countries including New Guinea, Jamaica, Peru, and Malawi.

Even though Brazil provides 30 percent of the world's coffee, more than 60 different species of coffee beans are grown in and shipped from a variety of countries. Consequently, many coffeehouses will concoct their own combinations of coffee blends, and will eagerly make a cappuccino or espresso with any bean of any flavor.

Coffee Drinks

Although the names and spelling for coffee drinks can be influenced by geographics (a German coffeehouse in Cozumel, Mexico called the Café Caribe offers a *capuchino*), there are different concoctions of espresso as well. *Espresso ristretto* is the same amount of coffee distilled into just less than 1 ounce of water, while an *espresso macchiato* is a shot of espresso "marked" with a tablespoon of frothed milk.

From Bean to Brew

Cappuccino is somewhat different from espresso. As legend has it, the Capuchin monks were quick to pick up the coffee habit because, during the long hours of prayer, the temptation to drift off was irresistible. Muslim traders brought them the Yemen Moka beans, roasted into an eye-opening brew that unfortunately was too strong—and bitter.

By way of a practical joke, a certain Brother Ibio was tripped while carrying a full bucket of sweet cream. The cream splashed into another brother's cup of coffee, and without noticing what had happened, the unsuspecting brother drank the coffee and cream mixture. The blend was much more pleasing, and thus the brothers found the perfect complement for their revitalizing brew.

Travelers who stopped to rest at the monastery shared in the monks' pleasure, and the word spread. Coincidentally, the Capuchin monks wore a brown habit topped with a white cowl, which resembled their beloved drink. Today, *cappuccino* consists of one-third espresso, one-third hot steamed milk, and one-third frothed milk.

Another coffee creation is *latte* (Italian for milk), which is reported to have been discovered by an Italian dairy farmer. His youngest son was ill, and the local custom was to give an excess of hot water to the infirm to "steam away the evil spirits." Being short on water, the farmer put milk in a kettle over the fire pit. The son drank his fill of the hot milk, and the farmer poured the remainder into his cup of coffee to avoid wasting it. Being pleased with the resulting mixture, he soon was sharing his new drink with his neighbors.

Today, latte is made with steamed milk and very little or no foam, and poured into a tall glass. A single espresso is slowly added and drifts to the bottom of the glass. The oils in the coffee determine where the mass is suspended. *Latte macchiato* consists of steamed and frothed milk marked with a tablespoon of espresso dripped through the foam.

Even though New Orleans is a major coffee importer, the types of coffee drinks are limited in comparison with other coffee consuming areas such as Seattle; Victoria, British Columbia; and Anchorage, Alaska. Macchiato is common in these places, as is *breve*, which uses half-and-half instead of regular whole, low-fat, or fat-free milk. Consequently, a customer would have no problem ordering a special combination such as a latte macchiato breve, which is extremely popular in Anchorage.

Although cappuccino was enjoyed in France, many Parisians desired a lighter drink for their breakfast meal. A milder brew was found by adding steamed milk to a half-cup of cappuccino, making *café au lait*. Some coffeehouses and restaurants today serve café au lait as a half-cup of regular brewed coffee and a half-cup of steamed milk.

Ice coffee is a phenomenon that has become quite popular—especially in warmer climates. Any coffee guide can describe the proper equipment and process for the "cold brew method," which uses devices such as the Toddy Coffee Maker, slowly dripping room-temperature water through grounds. It should be noted, however, that some houses will make ice coffee by pouring hot espresso over ice, which provides a totally different beverage than cold brew coffee.

Prior to the turn of the century, it was discovered that liquor could be mixed successfully, and tastefully, with coffee. New Orleans, ever the party town, developed an alcoholic coffee drink as far back as the 1890s. "Café Brûlot Diabolique" was created by Jules Alciatore and served at Antoine's restaurant. It contained a flaming mixture of coffee, brandy, and spices. This drink later became a popular way to disguise alcohol during Prohibition.

The Coffee Market

Gourmet coffee consumption has caught on so well in the U.S. that curbside cappuccino—made from such trendy blends as Sumatran, Ethiopian, and Costa Rican—are dispensed from $2,900 Italian-made Caramali espresso machines mounted on $13,000 push carts. Vendors with such high-end equipment can be found on streets in Manhattan recognized for high pedestrian traffic, and is so popular that the whole business seems unaffected by New York laws attempting to crack down on sidewalk vendors.

Seattle as well appears to be immune to legal harassment in the curbside vending business. There is a coffee cart within arm's reach on any given sidewalk in downtown Seattle, one or two on select street corners, parked outside grocery stores, and in the shopping malls of suburbia.

One retail chain even operates two kinds of stores. One store is a fast-paced espresso bar where coffee is poured from patented beer-like taps. Another store serves coffee by the cup, offers counter seating, and sells fresh coffee beans and brewing gear such as the cafetiere pot, espresso and cappuccino machines, and French coffee jugs.

An enterprising couple in New Orleans fashioned a coffee vehicle by converting a van into a mobile coffee counter that can park downtown in a variety of areas noted for heavy foot traffic. Celebrities, as well, are cashing in on this new wave of specialized socializing; actress Glenn Close, her sister Jessie, and writer Barbara Moss once owned the Leaf & Bean in Bozeman, Montana.

It is believed that this craze actually may have started in Seattle in Pike Place Market amid produce stall proprietors, fish market workers, and craftspeople. Sidewalk cafés in

Pioneer Square may offer such interesting blends as Guatemalan Antigua and Ethiopian Yergacheffe for a tangy espresso, while traditional coffee shops may still exist in such areas as First Avenue among the eclectic mix of business suits and Birkenstocks.

Even though coffee drinking is most often thought of as a relaxing social diversion, as a commercial venture the coffeehouse is a serious business. The Specialty Coffee Association of America (SCAA) is one of three trade organizations in the U.S. concerned with coffee, and specifically with specialty coffee. As part of SCAA affiliation, members can tour coffee-growing countries to get firsthand information about the coffee industry. The SCAA also hopes to establish technical standards for roasting and brewing coffee.

Consumption

According to the National Coffee Association 1997 Winter Coffee Drinking Study, 49 percent of the United States' population drinks coffee daily, with men drinking 1.7 cups to 1.5 cups for women. But only 37 percent drink their coffee black while as many as 63 percent add a sweetener and/or cream, milk, or a non-dairy substitute.

It may seem unusual that coffeehouses have proliferated in a city like New Orleans, known probably as one of the most popular party towns in the Northern Hemisphere. In the past several years, though, the coffeehouse scene has experienced dramatic growth here.

Even though the people of Finland are presently, per capita, the largest group of coffee consumers in the world, according to syndicated market research of grocery store sales, New Orleanians consume 1.5 times more coffee than the average city-dweller. And the coffee is brewed stronger here as well. The average consumer in other states will use about 1.5 ounces of coffee to make a standard pot, while coffee lovers in Louisiana use at least twice that much to brew the same amount.

To keep up with this demand, approximately 241,000 tons of coffee moved through the Port of New Orleans in 1995. That is 27.8 percent of all coffee that entered the U.S. that year, making one of the largest hauls of any port in the U.S., the Ports of New York and New Jersey being first and second, respectively, in 1989 and 1990. In 1991, the Port of New Orleans moved to first place as shown in table 3 below.

COFFEE HANDLING (1991)		
City	Tonnage	Bags
New Orleans	322,000	5,499,858
New York	212,438	3,628,498
San Francisco	145,130	2,478,870

Table 3. Coffee Handling (1991)

As can be seen, New Orleans is responsible for handling a fairly sizeable share of the beans shipped into American ports. And it should not be surprising that a portion of this haul stayed in New Orleans to supply one of the best-known coffee centers in the world.

Consequently, to keep flavor and freshness to an optimum, much coffee is roasted in the nine plants in and around New Orleans. At the time of this writing, these roasting plants include PJ's Coffee and Tea Company; Folger Coffee Company; Luzianne Coffee Company; Nestlé/Hills Brothers Coffee Company; International

Coffee Corporation; Coffee Roasters of New Orleans; Try-Me Coffee Mills; Covington Coffee Works; and Community Coffee Company, a distributor that also roasts their beans in a plant in Port Allen, Louisiana for their CC's Gourmet Coffee House chain.

The recent development and opening of a bulk handling plant in New Orleans may help this city maintain its status of being a top coffee port in the country. As of May 1993, New Orleans now operates the first, largest, and most versatile U.S. bulk coffee handling plant in the world— Silocaf of New Orleans, Inc.

Currently, 100,000 pounds of beans an hour slide across the conveyors at Silocaf. Here, both old and new forms of shipment are used: traditional bags that hold either 132 pounds or 154 pounds, the relatively new 2,000-pound plastic super sacks, and the 15-ton cargo containers protected by a plastic liner. And 203 bins hold a maximum capacity of 90 million pounds of beans. A similar bulk handling operation in Trieste, Italy has a capacity of about 20 million pounds in bins. The New Orleans plant processed 241,000 tons of beans in 1995 alone.

As a commercial venture, however, overconfidence in the coffee industry should be avoided. Even though the National Coffee Association says that nationwide, total coffee sales reach about $6.5 billion a year, some experts say that the business already is only a shadow of what it once was. There once were coffee traders up and down Magazine and Gravier streets in New Orleans, but today many of them are gone, having been replaced by large European companies with offices in New York.

The head of a New Orleans coffee association explains that national consumption is flat, if not losing ground. He gives such reasons as health concerns, coupled with the growing popularity of teas, designer soft drinks, and other beverages. Per capita, coffee consumption has been declining for more than 20 years, and the only segment of the market that is showing any growth is specialty coffees, with numerous coffeehouses springing up throughout the city and suburbs.

Perhaps one of New Orleans' first tastes of mainstream commercial gourmet-quality coffee was made available in the early 1990s when an ex-Starbucks roastmaster moved to the city and opened The Daily Planet Espresso Bar near Tulane University. Since then, Barnes and Noble bookstore in the New Orleans suburb of Metairie was one of the first venues to actually feature Starbucks coffee, and this was followed by the Starbucks company, which set up its first coffeehouse in late 1998 in Uptown New Orleans.

Proliferation of Coffeehouses

The number of coffeehouses has increased dramatically in New Orleans in the past several years, offering ambiance ranging from a form of neo-beatnik to a European-style slickness. There could be several reasons for this growth phenomenon.

Some say that patrons are attracted to the casual, and sometimes seedy, atmosphere of coffeehouses, particularly the venues considered by purists to be authentic because they serve coffee and tea only, as opposed to the homogenized, suburban, and sometimes more expensive businesses that simply put the words "coffeehouse," "coffee shop," "café," or "bistro" in the establishment's name. Also, the coffeehouse seems to be a result of neo-prohibitionism among younger adults who prefer this alternative to nightclubs as social meeting places.

Coffee seems to be more socially acceptable than alcohol because if too much caffeine is consumed, socially unacceptable behavior does not usually follow as with alcohol. Large amounts of coffee can be consumed, and the drinker will only feel tense. Consequently, older singles seem to appreciate the opportunity to meet other "sober" singles.

Some coffeehouses have a variety of attractions such as being combined with a bookstore as well as having pastries baked on the premises. Some creative establishments, such as Coffee Bean, The European Coffee House in Metairie, Louisiana, use their many square feet of floor space as a bookstore, restaurant, and coffeehouse, while others such as Cyrano's in Anchorage, Alaska add a theatrical playhouse and art film theater.

Another twist in an attempt to satiate the public's desire for gourmet coffee in an already relaxed atmosphere is the addition of a coffeehouse to a bookstore instead of the other way around. While Barnes and Noble Café features Starbucks coffee, Borders has its Espresso Bar, and Books-A-Million has Joe Mugg's Café.

Where music is concerned, New Orleanians are open to any opportunity to play or listen to original works. The more progressive coffeehouses inherently have provided an outlet for beginning musicians to show their talent, and occasionally some performers make it to the big time.

For example, Emily Salliers of the folk group Indigo Girls gave musical performances at the Penny Post Coffeehouse in New Orleans early in her career. And audiences at Lena Spencer's Caffè Lena in Saratoga Springs, New York experienced the early works of such icons as Arlo Guthrie, Bob Dylan, Spalding Gray, David Bromberg, and Bruce (Utah) Phillips.

In New Orleans, it seems ironic that a place known for its slow pace and southern flair for the low-pressure, easygoing lifestyle can be such a large consumer of a powerful stimulant like coffee. But perhaps one possible reason for the growth of this industry is that startup costs for a coffeehouse are about one-third that of opening a full-service restaurant with a license that allows grilling, frying, or liquor sales.

Moreover, this rapid growth may be compared with the influx of local comedy clubs of the past. But unlike the comedy club endeavors in New Orleans, the coffeehouse appears to be a more attractive—and stable—business venture, though, since it seems to offer a service more readily appreciated and sought after almost everywhere.

Perhaps another reason for the influx of coffeehouses is that traditional restaurants may frown on students, artists, and the after-theater crowd who want only dessert and coffee. Coffeehouses, on the other hand, take advantage of its patrons' love of eating; homemade pastries probably are as big an enticement as are the coffees themselves, and some establishments even go as far as to have these delicacies supplied to them directly by pastry chefs.

Moreover, there exists another class of people who simply want a place to study, write, or conduct other business, and not necessarily in private but surrounded by the eclectic, and sometimes eccentric, mix of others. And these students learn quickly which coffeehouses allow them to plug in a laptop computer.

Some establishment owners and managers prohibit the use of computers, claiming that the PCs drain too much power. But a more realistic reason may be that these proprietors do not want patrons occupying a table for hours on end while nursing a single cup of coffee. Starbucks, on the other hand, not only welcome laptop users, they also provide telephone lines for Internet access throughout some stores.

Some enterprising entrepreneurs, however, have

recognized this need and have developed "cyber cafés." These are coffeehouses that have installed high-speed dedicated line Internet accounts and a number of computer workstations. They charge customers for online time to access the Internet or email. But these Internet cafés often only specialize in either good espresso or good computer equipment; an establishment with both is a good find.

Yet another possible reason for the growth of coffeehouses, in New Orleans in particular, could be its ability to receive imports, via rail, highway, and waterway. As with any business dependant on logistics, the more accessible the supplies, the better potential for economic success.

The social significance of the coffeehouse may be equal to the significance of the coffee itself. The coffeehouse provides what sociologists call "third places," i.e., spots to gather away from home and work. That is the whole idea behind some of these meeting places: you go in and read the paper or a magazine in an environment that is conducive to casual conversation with strangers. Coffeehouses provide an experience beyond just drinking coffee: we like to drink it with others.

Whatever the reason for the growing number of coffeehouses, this business seems to have found its niche— one carved into a society that thrives on social interaction and a taste for the exotic.

From Bean to Brew

References

Arceneaux, Robert. Telephone conversation with author. New Orleans, LA, 11 December 1992.

Barlow, Yvonne. "Espresso on the Run." *Travel-Holiday* February 1989: 100.

Bell, Lydia. "Vienna, Mozart and More in Austria's Capital City." *Times-Picayune* [New Orleans, LA] 24 November 1991: E1, E4 Living.

Benning, Lee Edwards. *The Cook's Tales, Origins of Famous Foods and Recipes*. The Globe Pequot Press, 1992: 155.

Bloom, Jeremy. "Café Society." *New York Times* 19 May 1991, late ed., sec. 2: 31.

Brown, Catherine. *Broths to Bannocks, Cooking in Scotland 1690 to the Present Day*. London: John Murray Ltd, 1991: 15, 24.

Caffè Lena. Dir. Stephen Trombley. Mirage-land/International Cinema, 1989. 60 min.

Calamuneri, Nino. Personal interview with author. New Orleans, LA, 2 May 1992.

Castille, Sandie. Telephone interview with author. New Orleans, LA, 24 October 1991.

Collingwood, Harris. "Curbside Coffee for New York's Bon Vivants." *Business Week* 25 July 1988: 41.

"Complaints Close Sidewalk." *Times-Picayune* [New Orleans, LA] 16 March 1992: A-11.

Cooper, Christopher. "Success is a Matter of Style." *Times-Picayune* [New Orleans, LA] 14 January 1992: A-4.

Drake, Brian. "Shoestring Film Turns Into a Hit." *New York Times* 7 August 1991: B3.

Dreher, Rod. "Filmmaker Linklater Scores Hit with Low-Budget 'Slacker'" *Morning Advocate* [Baton Rouge, LA] 13 September 1991: 1C-2C.

Dunn, Debra. Personal interview with author. New Orleans, LA, 9 February 1991.

Finn, Kathy. "New Coffee Plant To Give N.O. a Lift; Italian Firm Will Turn Old Silo Into Nation's Top Processing Center." *CityBusiness* [New Orleans, LA] 2-15 December 1991: 1, 20.

Hall, John. "Yes! Dupuy Knows Beans About Coffee." *Times-Picayune* [New Orleans, LA] 12 April 1992: F-1, 4.

Jurich, Nick. *Espresso. From Bean to Cup.* Missing Link Press, 1991: 198 pps.

Keister, Kim. "New Orleans Comeback." *Historic Preservation* January/February 1991: 31+.

Know Your Coffee: A Nestlé Foodservice Guide. Nestlé Foodservice, Croyden, England, 1991: 2.

Kutner, Sanford A. "Grandma Ruth—85 and Working Every Day!!!" *This Week In New Orleans* August 8, 1992: 1.

Laun, Kathleen. "A Lot Goes Into That Cup of Jo Before It Reaches Your Table." *Times-Picayune* [New Orleans, LA] 11 October 1992: 20-21, 40.

Lemann, Bernard, Samuel Wilson, Jr. *Architectural Inventory.* New Orleans: Pelican Publishing Company, Inc., 1971: 136. Vol. 1 of *New Orleans Architecture.* 2 vols.

Louis, David. *2201 Fascinating Facts.* New York: Greenwich House, 1983: 86.

Manger, René. *Spilling the Beans* Vol. I, Issue 12, August 21, 1992.

———. *Spilling the Beans* Vol. II, Issue 3, November 27, 1992.

Marsh, Michael. Personal interview with author. New Orleans, LA, 9 February 1991.

Molloy, Joanna. "Hot Coffee: Beauties of the Night on Union Square." *New York* 13 August 1990: 40, 43.

Mullener, Elizabeth. "Glory Days: Magazine Street

Coming Back." *Times-Picayune* [New Orleans, LA] 15 January 1992: A-9.

Olson, Alison. "Coffee House Lobbying." *History Today* January 1991: 35-41.

Owen, Thompson, Steve Hamilton, Ted Hood. *Uncommon Grounds, A Publication of Kaldi's Coffeehouse and Coffeemuseum* March 1992: 1-9.

Pacorini, Massimo. Fax to author. Silocaf, New Orleans, LA, 12 December 1996.

Paulsen, Eric. "Seattle's Coffee Subculture." *ITN, The Newsletter of the International Television Association* April 1992: 10, 12.

Reiking, Herta. Personal interview with author. Cozumel, Mexico, 13 August 1992.

Roppolo, Jerry. Personal interview with author. New Orleans, LA, 9 February 1991.

Slacker. Dir. Richard Linklater. 16 mm, 97 min. 1989. Detour, Inc.

Snow, Constance. "Café Olé!" *Times-Picayune* [New Orleans, LA] 23 August 1991: 18-20 Lagniappe.

———. "Some Hot Spots for the Coffee Crowd." *Times-Picayune* [New Orleans, LA] 2 November 1990: 33-34 Lagniappe.

Street, Julia. "Dear Julia." *New Orleans Magazine* March 1993: 14.

Vogt, Jenny. "Caffeine Overload May Be Last Socially Acceptable Vice." *Times-Picayune* [New Orleans, LA] 24 September 1991: 1-2 Living.

Voelker, Bill. "Businesswomen Take Gamble on Coffeehouse." *Times-Picayune* [New Orleans, LA] 20 August 1992: D-1, D-2.

Welsh, James. "Ahhhhhh, Coffee." *Times-Picayune* [New Orleans, LA] 21 February 1993: F-1, F-2.

Williams, David. Email to author. Port of New Orleans,

From Bean to Brew

New Orleans, LA, 11 December 1996.

Wintergreen, Donna. "Café Society." *Restaurant Hospitality* May 1990: 132-134.

Zimmerman, Curtis. Telephone conversation with author. New Orleans, LA, 11 December 1992.

Contacts

Best Investments
Daily Coffee Newsletter
www.binews.com

Café Magazine
P.O. Box 173
Cambridge CB5 8YB
England
CafeMagazine@blackapollo.com
www.blackapollo.demon.co.uk/2cafindex.html

Coffee Review
600 Townsend Street, Suite 135E
San Francisco, CA 94103
415-522-5380
415-522-5383 fax
editor@coffeereview.com
www.coffeereview.com

Epicure Exchange
3333 24th Street
San Francisco, CA 94110
650.964.6666
www.epicure.com

International Coffee Organization
22 Berners Street
London W1P 4DD
England
44 (0)20 7580 8591
44 (0)20 7580 6129
info@ico.org
www.ico.org

From Bean to Brew

Lucidcafé
1825 Winchester Blvd.
Campbell, CA 95008
408-871-9270
robin@lucidcafe.com
www.lucidcafe.com/lucidcafe

National Coffee Association of America
Coffee Science Source
15 Maiden Lane
New York, NY 10038
212-344-5596
212-425-7059 fax
info@coffeescience.org
www.coffeescience.org

Specialty Coffee Association of America
One World Trade Center, Suite 1200
Long Beach, CA 90831-1200
562-624-4100
562-624-4101 fax
coffee@scaa.org
www.scaa.org

Index

6

8

9

C

D

E

Y